The smart investor:

A perfect guide to intelligent and successful investing

Donna A. Henderson

All rights reserved. No part of this publication may be reproduced, distributed, or transmitted in any form or by any means, including photocopying, recording, or other electronic or mechanical methods, without the prior written permission of the publisher, except in the case of brief quotations embodied in critical reviews and certain other noncommercial uses permitted by copyright law.
Copyright © Donna A. Henderson, 2022.

Table of contents

[Chapter 1](#)
[Chapter 2](#)
[Chapter 3](#)
[Chapter 4](#)
[Chapter 5](#)
[Chapter 6](#)
[Chapter 7](#)
[Chapter 8](#)
[Chapter 9](#)
[Chapter 10](#)
[Chapter 11](#)
[Chapter 12](#)
[Chapter 13](#)
[Chapter 14](#)
[Chapter 15](#)
[Chapter 16](#)

Chapter 1

The most effective method to set up your own monetary arrangement

What is a Financial Plan?
A monetary arrangement is a guide for an individual or an organization to arrive at its objectives.
It considers what is happening and objectives, then, at that point, comes up with a definite methodology in view of your focus on goals, telling you precisely where to spend your cash, and when to save.

Furthermore, monetary plans assist you with planning for the unforeseen by having you saved a pot of cash. At the point when a surprising employment cutback, sickness or monetary slump happens, you can depend on these assets to cover your everyday costs.

With regards to your cash and your arrangements, it tends to be difficult to adjust momentary needs, long haul dreams, and those surprising occasions that are beyond your control.

From some basic foods you want, to the retirement you need, and the vehicle fix charge that is approaching, it very well may be difficult to sort out some way to handle bills simultaneously you plan for the future. Making a monetary arrangement could give you more certainty with your money. In addition, it implies less evenings agonizing over those troublesome bills.

The difficulty is many individuals don't have the foggiest idea where to begin. They stress over things like "how much does a monetary arrangement cost?" and expect they need perpetual expert help.

The uplifting news? It's rarely past the point of no return (or too soon) to begin dealing with your monetary arrangement. Far superior - making a monetary arrangement isn't generally so convoluted as you'd suspect. You might actually separate it into simple tasks, similar to this:

Step 1: Review what is happening
Before you start the real arranging part of the cycle, you really want to know where your process will begin. That implies looking at what your monetary circumstance resembles at the present time.

Truly, everybody could profit from putting resources into additional regular monetary exams, however putting off taking a gander at your bank statements is simple.

Consider it - when's the last time you really took a gander at each of your installments for gas, power, broadband, and Netflix, and sorted out what they amount to?

Get your last 6 to a year of bank proclamations and feature each normal active cost in one tone, then feature your unpredictable costs in another.

It may very well be useful to order these expenses into individual and "urgent" costs. Whenever you have all the right data before you, ask yourself:

- Where might I at any point eliminate spending?

- What amount might I at any point save by changing to an alternate help?
- Do I truly require all of my "discretionary" costs?

Step 2: Set present moment and long haul objectives
Presently you have a beginning stage for your excursion to independence from the rat race.

The following stage is sorting out where you're going. This is a significant part in your monetary arrangement for fakers venture.

Laying out strong objectives provides you guidance and clearness while arriving at conclusions about your funds. Your objectives will show you on the off chance that you're moving in the correct bearing.

Preferably, you'll require your objectives to be S.M.A.R.T. This implies they're:

- Specific
- Measurable
- Attainable
- Relevant
- Time-bound

Try not to simply say you need to have more cash in your reserve funds. Record an explanation that makes sense of precisely exact thing you need to achieve, for example,

"I need to have something like $2,000 in my bank account toward the following year's end."

Transient monetary objectives, similar to "I'll put $100 in my reserve funds one month from now", keep you persuaded by showing steady advancement. Long haul objectives provide you with more predictable guidance to move in.

Stage 3: Create an arrangement for your obligations
Nobody likes contemplating obligations - except for these are issues that you can't overlook to be monetarily keen.
Individual monetary plans can help.

You can't gain a gigantic headway with your short and long haul objectives in the event that your advantage and reimbursements are overloading you. So sort out some way to pay what you owe first.

Begin by making an arrangement to dispose of your most hazardous obligations. These are the costs that cost the most because of exorbitant financing costs and expenses. Dispose of those as quick as possible.

Assuming you're battling to deal with a few obligations on the double, it could assist with seeing whether you can solidify everything into one, less expensive credit.

The main concern is you want to make a move and begin pursuing being sans obligation. Keep in mind, obligations incorporate everything from quick issues, similar to charge cards, to long haul costs, similar to understudy obligation.

Stage 4: Establish your rainy day account
A backup stash resembles a monetary wellbeing cover.

Regardless of how "ready" you assume you are, there's dependably an opportunity that some surprising expense will come and deeply inspire you.

Crisis reserves safeguard you against things like startling disease, out of nowhere losing your employment, or even a bill that you neglected to pay.

While the specific measure of crisis financing you have relies upon you, it ought to by and large cover around 3 to a half year of your proper costs. You can likewise save to the point of covering variable costs like diversion and food as well.

Crisis reserves are gainful for anybody. Nonetheless, they're especially significant in the event that you're a specialist, somebody with an unfortunate FICO rating, or somebody with variable pay.

While setting up your own monetary plans, ensure you have a backup stash set up.

Stage 5: Start domain arranging
Domain arranging is one of those convoluted terms that the vast majority overlook - accepting it just applies to well off individuals, or individuals moving toward retirement.

Nonetheless, it's fundamental that you ponder safeguarding your family when you're nowhere to be found. A legitimate home arrangement gives you all out inward feeling of harmony.

Domain plans include:

- Last will and confirmation
- Medical care mandates
- Overarching legal authority
- Trust data

This report could likewise incorporate different provisions for things like last attitude guidelines and guardianship assignments.

Home arranging probably won't be everything thing you can manage with your Friday night fun-wise, however it will guarantee that you're safeguarded for anything.

Stage 6: Begin putting resources into your future

The subsequent stage is creating anything financial wellbeing you as of now have, so you're arranged for what's to come. You can start zeroing in on your reserve funds and making speculations.

You could have various designs to suit your present moment and long haul objectives. For example, your momentary monetary arrangement could cover the means you will take to create financial stability now. Your 5-year monetary arrangement could see things like retirement.

Contributing for retirement is one of the most outstanding ways of guaranteeing that you're prepared to handle what's in store. At the point when you start making arrangements for retirement, you'll have to consider a couple of factors like:

Wanted retirement age: When might you want to quit working (be sensible here)
Wanted way of life: What sort of way of life do you need? Do you believe that enough money should do anything you like? Then plan for that!
Current wellbeing: Health is certainly a major supporter of riches. Assuming you know medical conditions are reasonable for you, prepare sure you're to handle the issue.
Reserve funds rate: How much are you saving towards the future at this moment

Assuming that you're fresh out of the plastic new to money management, search out some additional help. There are abundance counselors out there that can acquaint you with various types of venture records and vehicles.

Stage 7: Get secured
Similarly as crisis reserves safeguard you from startling amazements throughout everyday life, protection shields your money from any unanticipated dangers.

Having the right protection implies that you won't have to continually break into your reserve funds each time something turns out badly. For example, home protection implies that you're appropriately safeguarded from things like cataclysmic events and break-ins.

Vehicle protection guarantees that assuming anything turns out badly with your vehicle, you're prepared to bounce in and fix the issue - without gigantic installments.

Having a secret stash and ensuring you're guaranteed appropriately implies that you can keep steady over the entirety of your investment funds objectives - in any event, whenever hard times arise.

Make a rundown of all the protection you could require while arranging monetary arrangement parts.

Stage 8: Keep track of your arrangement
The significance of a monetary arrangement is something you can't stand to misjudge.

The more you are familiar with your ongoing monetary circumstance and where you're going, the more certain you'll spend.

Notwithstanding, getting a monetary arrangement model format and building your own technique is only the principal leg of the excursion. You additionally need to focus on effectively keeping tabs on your development.

Really look at it like clockwork or somewhere in the vicinity, and ensure you're moving in the correct bearing. A great deal can change in your monetary circumstance inside only half a month.

Make sure to refresh your arrangement when huge occasions happen in your life as well. Having a kid, getting hitched, or buying another home will all make new contemplations for you to think about.

Effectively surveying and refreshing your arrangement implies that you can partake in an impenetrable system for arriving at your monetary objectives.

Chapter 2

Elements to consider when investing in stocks

At the point when you choose to purchase a stock for effective financial planning, it is vital to get your work done as you are putting your well deserved cash into it. Your objective ought to find great worth particularly when you are purchasing a stock as long as possible.

Yet, before you put your full confidence in an organization, you ought to do exhaustive exploration, examine stock's essentials and check if that stock fits in your portfolio prior to purchasing a stock.

You are purchasing a stock as well as you are turning into an investor of that organization, so as an investor you ought to do the legitimate examination.

Here are key elements you ought to realize about an organization prior to purchasing a stock and putting away your well deserved cash.

1. Time Skyline:
You, first and foremost, need to conclude the time skyline prior to purchasing a stock as it assumes a significant part in choosing whether to purchase that stock or not. Your effective money management time skyline can be present moment, center term or long haul, in view of your monetary objectives.

Momentary A transient time skyline is any speculation that you are intending to claim for or under one year. In the event that you're wanting to purchase a stock and hold it for under a year, then it is ideal to put resources into stable blue-chip stocks which deliver profits. The organizations have a decent monetary record and there are less dangers implied.

Medium Term-A medium-term venture is a speculation that you need to hold from one year to 10 years. For center terms one ought to put resources into quality developing business sectors endlessly stocks having a moderate degree of chance.
Long haul At last, long haul ventures are any speculation that you are intending to clutch for over 10 years. These have opportunity and energy to recuperate on the off chance that something turns out badly and can produce a critical return.

2. Speculation Procedure:
Prior to purchasing a stock, it is vital to concentrate on different money

management methodologies and pick the one which suits your financial planning style

The following are three critical kinds of techniques that are utilized by best investors:

Esteem Effective money management: Worth putting is the sort of putting resources into stocks that are underestimated contrasted with their friends in order to produce gains. This is the methodology that is utilized by Warren Buffett to create gigantic gains.

Development Contributing: Development putting is the sort of putting resources into stocks that show market-beating development concerning income and profit. Development investors accept that the vertical patterns in these stocks will proceed and set out a freedom to produce benefits.

Pay Financial planning: At long last, investors ought to search for quality stocks that deliver huge profits. These profits create pay that can be utilized or reinvested for expanding income potential. Hence, prior to purchasing a stock, you ought to consider the technique that fits in well with that contributing style.

3. Investor Example:
investors ought to check the shareholding design prior to purchasing a stock.

Advertisers are substances that impact an organization. They might have a gigantic controlling stake in the organization or stand firm on senior leader situations.

Subsequently, investors ought to put resources into those organizations having a high advertiser holding, High Homegrown Institutional investor holding and furthermore High Unfamiliar Institutional investor holding.

4. Size of the Organization:
The size of the organization that you are thinking about putting resources into assumes a vital part in how much gamble that you need to take for purchasing a stock.

In this manner it is vital to consider the organization's size contrasted with your gamble resistance and time skyline prior to purchasing a stock.

The size of public corporations is not entirely set in stone by checking out the organization's market capitalization.

5. Income Development:
Prior to purchasing a stock, investors ought to see those organizations that are developing. This is still up in the air by actually looking at the two its income and its profit.

Chapter 3

Things investors should be familiar with about their portfolio

Beginning your way to fruitful financial planning could appear to be overpowering, yet there's a compelling reason needed to stress. A huge number of individuals have ventured to every part of a similar street as they cleared their path through wins and fails, war and harmony, significant life altering situations, and each diversion life can toss at you. With tolerance, discipline, and a feeling of quiet, you can endure the hardship and dominate the competition. The following are a couple of things to remember as you move toward effective money management and monetary achievement.

1. Exploit the Force of Compounding

You might have heard this multiple times, yet you must genuinely assimilate it such that it changes your way of behaving and reorders your needs. You will wind up far more extravagant on the off chance that you start effective money management early. It's everything because of compound returns, and the result differentials are faltering.

For instance, a 18-year-old who bounces straight into the labor force and saves $5,000 each year in an expense sanctuary like a Roth IRA, procuring long haul normal paces of return, could wind up resigning with $4,359,874. For a 38-year-old to accomplish exactly the same thing, they would have to save more than $36,000 each year. A school graduate could wind up with $4,426,000 by saving $111 per check all through their lifetime. Everything reduces to utilizing the time worth of cash.

2. Tailor Your Portfolio to Your Remarkable Life Conditions

Individuals will quite often get sincerely engaged with their speculations and are at times excessively joined to a specific lawful design, technique, or organization. They lose their objectivity and fail to remember the aphorism "Assuming it looks unrealistic, it most likely is."

Be attentive on the off chance that you go over pitches like these:

The main stock you'll at any point have to purchase.

Purchase these three file reserves. Furthermore, disregard all the other things.

Global stocks are in every case better compared to homegrown stocks.

You have something important to take care of as the director of your portfolio. That occupation relies upon many variables, including your own objectives, risk-resilience level, targets, assets, personality, mental profile, charge section, eagerness to commit time, and even biases. At last, your portfolio ought to assume the engraving of your character and extraordinary circumstances throughout everyday life.

Contributing personas are basically as shifted as individual investors. For instance, a well off, previous confidential financier who is fit for perusing a pay explanation and monetary record might need to gather a six-figure recurring, automated revenue from profits, interest, and leases coming about because of having assembled an assortment of blue-chip stocks, overlaid edged bonds, and prize business structures. In correlation, a youthful laborer might need to purchase the least expensive, most enhanced, most duty effective assortment of stocks through a minimal expense record store in their 401(k). A widow who is uncertain of financial exchange accidents might need to procure an arrangement of money creating investment properties with excess supports stopped in testaments of the store.

None of these choices is off-base or better than the others. The inquiry is whether the portfolio, strategy, and holding structure are ideal for anything that objective the individual needs to accomplish.

3. Get ready To Experience Drops in Market Worth

Resource costs are continuously moving. Once in a while these developments are unreasonable, like market disturbance from Holland's tulip bulbs, and here and there they are brought about by macroeconomic occasions. For example, you could see a mass markdown of stocks because of enormous venture banks plunging toward insolvency. These banks would have to sell everything they can, as fast as possible, to raise cash, regardless of whether they realize the resources are very reasonable. Land costs likewise vary, with costs going down, then returning up.

However long you have fabricated your portfolio astutely, the fundamental possessions are supported by genuine procuring power, and you bought resources at sensible costs, you ought to be fine.

The Dow Jones Modern Normal fell 34.6% from August 1987 to December 1987. It dropped 34.4% from Walk 2000 to October 2002, then, at that point, rose 94.4% by October 2008. Among then, at that point, and Walk 2009, value costs declined 53.8%.[1]

In the event that you are a drawn out investor with a sensible future, you will encounter these drops at least a time or two. You might watch your $500,000 portfolio decline to $250,000 — regardless of whether it is loaded up with your thought process. These are the most secure, most expanded stocks and bonds. A great deal of mix-ups are made — and cash lost — by attempting to stay away from the unavoidable.

4. Pay a Certified Counsel to Work With You

Before the ascent of conducting financial matters, it was accepted that the vast majority pursued judicious monetary choices. Studies created by the scholar, monetary, and speculation areas throughout the course of recent many years showed how wrong that expectation ended up being concerning true results for investors.

Except if individuals have the information, experience, premium, and personality to overlook the market's intrinsic vacillations, they will generally do a few stupid things. These missteps incorporate pursuing execution by tossing cash into resources that have as of late expanded in cost. One more model is selling top notch possessions at absolute bottom costs during monetary misery.

Alternately, investors who pay a counselor sensible expenses, so another person is accomplishing the work for them, have obviously better certifiable results, in spite of the additional charge cost.

All in all, exemplary financial experts missed the point entirely, including a portion of the great clerics of minimal expense effective money management, for example, John Bogle, who established

Vanguard. Incidentally, a investor's return was not just the consequence of gross returns short expenses, with paid guides removing esteem. All things being equal, consultants procured their expenses, frequently in spades. A normal investor could wind up with a lot more significant yields on the grounds that a guide held their hand and changed their way of behaving.

5. Utilize Duty and Resource Assurance Procedures

It's feasible for two individuals with indistinguishable saving and ways of managing money and similar arrangement of stocks, securities, common assets, and land to wind up with ridiculously various measures of abundance, contingent upon how they organized their property.

From basic procedures, for example, resource situation and utilizing customary or Roth IRAs, to further developed ideas, for example, setting up a family restricted association to decrease gift charges, it is beneficial to get familiar with the guidelines, guidelines, and regulations, and to apply them to your advantage.

For example, you might be qualified for limitless chapter 11 insurance of the resources held inside the bounds of specific kinds of records. On the off chance that you end up confronting chapter 11, your most memorable strategy ought to be to talk with a legal counselor. They could direct you to bow out of all financial obligations and begin once again. You could wind up leaving the town hall with most, or all, of your retirement plan resources flawless, proceeding to build returns for you as they siphon out profits, interest, and leases.

6. Know the 3 Ways to deal with Getting Resources

Eventually, there are just three different ways you can secure resources. Whether they work relies upon how much money management wise you have.

Orderly Buys

You make orderly buys when you routinely trade portions of an assortment of resources over the long haul, paying little heed to valuation, expecting to adjust the great and terrible times. It is for individuals who would rather not invest a great deal of energy contemplating their portfolios. All things being equal, they let expansion, minimal expense and long haul uninvolved possession, and time accomplish basically everything for them.

Valuation

Valuation contributing is trading in view of value, comparative with the moderately assessed characteristic worth of a resource. This technique requires huge information on business, bookkeeping, money, and financial matters. It expects you to assess resources as though you were a confidential purchaser.

Many individuals have developed well off along these lines, as well. Graham terms the individual who involves this methodology as the "Venturesome investor." They need to control risk, partake in an edge of wellbeing, and realize that there are adequate profit and resources comparative with the cost paid for each situation in their portfolio.

This technique is for the investor who needs to nod off around evening time without stressing whether the nation will encounter another 1929 — 33 or 1973 — 74 market decline. As a matter of fact, the whole monetary framework lays on this technique. This is on the grounds that costs can veer off from the hidden reality for just so lengthy.

Practically all high-profile investors who have great long haul records fall into this camp, including the individuals who have turned into a voice for the main methodology. This rundown incorporates Vanguard pioneer Bogle. He exchanged an enormous piece of his stock property during the website blast in light of the fact that the yield on the stocks had become little comparative with the yield accessible on U.S. Depository bonds at that point.

Market Timing
At long last, there is the market-timing investor, who trades in light of what they think the securities exchange or economy will do within a reasonable time-frame.

Market timing is a type of hypothesis. A couple of individuals have gotten rich off of it, at the same time, as is normally done, it isn't manageable. The not so distant future is unseeable in light of the fact that it is what's to come.

On the off chance that you are another investor, adhere to the main strategy. On the off chance that you become a specialist, adhere to the subsequent technique. Furthermore, despite the fact that it sells well, individuals with good judgment ought to keep away from the third technique.

Chapter 4

Things to consider when selecting stock

Stock investors face a tough challenge in choosing where to invest. Reviewing the massive amount of data available on public companies is vital for assessing the quality of companies and determining whether they're suitable for their portfolios. But, it can be an arduous process.

When you're evaluating something like bonds, the overriding consideration is credit quality. With stocks, there's no such silver bullet. So individual investors interested in buying equities are faced with a much tougher task: performing personal due diligence or, if they have advisors, evaluating their recommendations.

The challenge lies in selecting the right information for assessing a specific stock and evaluating it correctly. The process of selecting what stocks to invest in can be simplified by using five basic evaluative criteria.

1. Good current and projected profitability. When choosing stocks, it's important to consider a company's financial fundamentals, including earnings, operating margins and cash flow. Together, these factors can paint a reasonable picture of the company's current financial health and how profitable it's likely to be in the near and long-term.

On the earnings side, investors should consider how stable those earnings are and how they're trending. Higher operating margins are typically more favorable than lower operating margins, in terms of measuring how efficiently a company operates. Reviewing the company's cash-flow figures, specifically cash flow per share, is helpful in gauging profitability. It's also a way to assess whether a stock is over- or undervalued.

2. Favorable asset utilization. Favorable asset utilization is the ratio of revenue earned for each dollar of assets a company owns. For example, if a company has an asset utilization ratio of 40 percent, it's earning 40 cents for each dollar of assets it owns. Different ratios are favorable in different industries. Similar to operating margin, the asset utilization ratio is a way to measure efficiency over time.

3. Conservative capital structure. Capital structure refers to how a company funds its business operations, using both debt

and equity. A conservative capital structure means that a company characteristically marshals capital in ways that create enough short-term liquidity to cover operating costs, while also reserving enough finance expansion without significantly increasing long-term debt.

4. Earnings momentum. Current or recent earnings, the fixation of many investors, are nothing more than snapshots of where a company is, or was, at a given point in time. To see where companies are likely headed, look for earnings momentum — the slowing or acceleration of earnings growth from one period to the next— as demonstrated by patterns.

Look for these patterns by examining earnings reports over the previous eight quarters, and reading analysts' projections for future earnings. If a company posted its best earnings of the last five years, two years ago, and has been lackluster since, it may be under increasing competitive pressure.

5. Intrinsic value (rather than market value). Intrinsic value is determined by analysts using complex absolute and relative valuation models. Available to individual investors online, these figures are a way to cut through market buzz to get a handle on a stock's real value.

In the short term, intrinsic value can vary significantly from market value, which is influenced by perception and behavioral investing factors. Ideally, you want stocks whose intrinsic value is higher than the market value, as this can suggest eventual price growth.

Chapter 5

The most effective method to manage market anomalies

  It is generally given that there are no complementary lifts or free snacks on Money Road. With many investors continually on the chase after even a small part of a percent of additional presentation, there are no simple methods for beating the market. By the way, certain tradable peculiarities appear to continue in the securities exchange, and those naturally entrance numerous investors.
While these irregularities merit investigating, investors ought to remember this mindfulness: Inconsistencies can show up, vanish, and return with basically no advance notice.

1. Little Firms Will quite often Beat
More modest firms (that is, more modest capitalization) will generally beat bigger organizations. As irregularities go, the little firm impact checks out. An organization's monetary development is eventually the main impetus behind its stock execution, and more modest organizations have significantly longer runways for development than bigger organizations.

An organization like Microsoft (MSFT) could have to find an extra $10 billion in deals to become 10%, while a more modest organization could require just an extra $70 million in deals for a similar development rate. Likewise, more modest firms ordinarily can develop a lot quicker than bigger organizations.

2. January Impact
The January impact is a somewhat notable peculiarity. Here, the thought is

that stocks that failed to meet expectations in the final quarter of the earlier year will generally beat the business sectors in January. The justification for the January impact is consistent to the point that calling it an anomaly is practically hard. investors will frequently hope to cast off failing to meet expected stocks late in the year so they can utilize their misfortunes to counterbalance capital increases charges (or to take the little derivation that the IRS permits assuming there is a net capital deficit for the year). Many individuals call this occasion charge misfortune reaping.

As selling pressure is once in a while free of the organization's genuine basics or valuation, this expense selling can push these stocks to levels where they become appealing to purchasers in January. Moreover, investors will frequently abstain from purchasing failing to meet expectations stocks in the final quarter and hold on until January to try not to become involved with the duty misfortune selling. Subsequently, there is overabundance selling tension before January and abundance purchasing strain after January 1, prompting this impact.

3. Low Book Worth

Broad scholarly exploration has shown that stocks with sub optimal cost to-book proportions will generally beat the market. Various test portfolios have shown that purchasing an assortment of stocks with low cost/book proportions will convey market-beating execution. Albeit this oddity sounds good to a point — surprisingly modest stocks ought to stand out for purchasers and return to the mean — this is, sadly, a generally powerless inconsistency. However the facts confirm that low cost-to-book stocks beat collectively, individual execution is particular, and it takes exceptionally huge arrangements of low cost-to-book stocks to see the advantages.

4. Disregarded Stocks
A nearby cousin of the little firm irregularity, purported dismissed stocks are likewise remembered to beat the expansive market midpoints. The ignored firm impact happens on stocks that are less fluid (lower exchanging volume) and will generally have insignificant expert help. The thought here is that as these organizations are found by investors, the stocks will beat.
Numerous investors screen long haul buying markers like P/E proportions and RSI. These let them know if a stock has been oversold, and on the off chance that it very well may be an ideal opportunity to think about stacking up on shares.

5. Inversions

Some proof recommends that stocks at one or the flip side of the exhibition range, over timeframes (by and large a year), will generally switch course in the accompanying time frame — the previous top entertainers become the upcoming underperformers, as well as the other way around.

In addition to the fact that measurable proof backs this up, yet the peculiarity likewise checks out as per venture essentials. Assuming a stock is a top entertainer on the lookout, chances are that its exhibition has made it costly; similarly, the opposite is valid for underperformers. Apparently like sound judgment, then, at that point, to expect that the overrated stocks would fail to meet expectations (aligning their valuation back) while the undervalued stocks beat.

Inversions additionally possible work to some degree since individuals anticipate that they should work. Assuming an adequate number of investors constantly sell last year's champs and purchase last year's washouts, that will assist with moving the stocks in the very expected headings, making it something of an unavoidable irregularity.

6. Days of the Week

Effective market allies disdain the times of the week irregularity since it has all the earmarks of being valid, however it additionally has neither rhyme nor reason. Research has shown that stocks will generally move more on Fridays than Mondays and that there is a predisposition toward positive market execution on Fridays. It's anything but an enormous inconsistency, yet it is a steady one.

On a key level, there is no great explanation for why this ought to be valid. A few mental variables could be working. Maybe a finish-of-week good faith saturates the market as dealers and investors anticipate the end of the week. On the other hand, maybe the end of the week allows investors an opportunity to get up to speed with their perusing, stew and worry about the market, and form negativity going into Monday.

7. Canines of the Dow
The Canines of the Dow are incorporated to act as an illustration of the risks of exchanging oddities. The thought behind this hypothesis was fundamentally that investors could beat the market by choosing stocks in the Dow Jones Modern Normal that had specific worth credits.
investors rehearsed various variants of the methodology, however there were

two normal methodologies. The first is to choose the 10 most elevated yielding Dow stocks. The subsequent technique is to go above and beyond and take the five stocks from that rundown with the most minimal outright stock cost and hold them for a year.

Chapter 6

Investment charges

Investing is a fabulous method for creating financial wellbeing and security, but at the same time it's an incredible method for making a strong bill in the event that you fail to see how and when the IRS forces charges on speculations.

Here are normal kinds of assessments on ventures and how you might limit what you owe.

1. Charge on capital additions
What it is: Capital increases are the benefits from the offer of a resource — portions of stock, a land parcel, a business — and by and large are viewed as available pay.

How it functions: The cash you make on the offer of any of these things is your capital addition. For instance, on the off chance that you sold a stock for a $10,000 benefit this year, you might need to pay capital increases charge on the increase. The rate you pay depends to some degree on how long you held the resource prior to selling. The duty rate on capital increases for most resources held for over one year is 0%, 15% or 20%. Capital increases charges on most resources held for under a year compare to normal personal expense rates.

Instructions to limit it: You can decrease capital additions charges on speculations by utilizing misfortunes to balance gains. This is called charge misfortune collecting. For instance, on the off chance that you sold a stock for a $10,000 benefit this year and sold one more at a

$4,000 misfortune, you'll be burdened on capital increases of $6,000.

2. Charge on profits

What it is: Profits for the most part are available pay in the year they're gotten. Regardless of whether you get a profit in real money — suppose you naturally reinvested yours to purchase more portions of the basic stock, for example, in a profit reinvestment plan (Dribble) — you actually need to report it.

How it functions: There are for the most part two sorts of profits: nonqualified and qualified. The expense rate on nonqualified profits is equivalent to your customary annual assessment section. The expense rate on qualified profits for the most part is lower: It's 0%, 15% or 20%, contingent upon your available pay and documenting status. After the year's end, you'll get a Structure 1099-DIV or a

Timetable K-1 from your dealer or any element that sent you something like $10 in profits and different circulations. The 1099-DIV shows what you were delivered and whether the profits were qualified or nonqualified.

Instructions to limit it: Holding ventures for a specific timeframe can qualify their profits for a lower charge rate. Making sure to save cash for the charges on profit installments can assist with staying away from a money crunch when the expense bill shows up, however holding profit paying ventures within a retirement record can be a method for conceding charges on speculations.

3. Charge on shared reserves
What it is: Common asset burdens ordinarily remember charges for profits and capital additions while you own the

asset shares, as well as capital increases charges when you sell the asset shares.

How it functions: Your common asset might produce and convey profits, premium or capital additions from the speculations inside the asset. As needs be, you might owe charges on these ventures — regardless of whether you haven't sold any of the offers or gotten any money from them. The expense rate you pay relies upon the sort of dispersion you get from the shared asset, as well as different variables. In the event that you sell your common asset shares for a benefit, you could cause capital additions charge.

Instructions to limit it: Holding up essentially a year to sell your portions could bring down your capital increases charge rate. Holding common asset shares inside a retirement record could concede the expense on the interest, profits or gains your common asset circulates. Charge misfortune reaping and picking reserves more averse to circulate available pay are different choices.

4. Charge on the offer of a house
What it is: In the event that you sell your home for a benefit, a portion of the addition could be available.

How it functions: The IRS normally permits you to avoid up to $250,000 of capital additions on your main living place in the event that you're single and $500,000 assuming you're hitched and recording mutually. Let's assume you and your life partner purchased a home a long time back for $200,000 and sold it today for $800,000. Assuming you record your duties mutually, $500,000 of that gain probably won't be dependent upon the capital additions charge (however $100,000 of the increase could be). What rate you pay on the other $100,000 would depend to some degree on your pay and your expense documenting status.

Instructions to limit it: You need to meet specific models to fit the bill for this prohibition, so make certain to survey them before you sell. You could fit the bill for a special case, and adding the worth of home upgrades you've made could help.

Chapter 7

Finding out about asset classes

What Is an Asset Class?

A resource class is a gathering of speculations that show comparative qualities and are dependent upon similar regulations and guidelines. Resource classes are in this way comprised of instruments that frequently act in basically the same manner to each other in the commercial center.

Sorts of resource classes
Here are the essential resource classes:

Cash and cash equivalents. You understand what money is — the lawful delicate we use to purchase products and pay obligations. Cash counterparts are speculations that can without much of a stretch be changed over into cash. Models incorporate currency market reserves and U.S. Depository bills and declarations of store (CDs) that full grown in three months or less.

Equities. Values are portions of proprietorship in an organization, otherwise called stock. The worth of values can rise or fall in light of the organization's exhibition, investor interest, and different variables. In a perfect world, stocks expansion in esteem after some time, making returns for investors. A few stocks likewise bring about profit installments.

Fixed income. Fixed-pay protections, or bonds, are advances that are separated into units and offered to investors. investors give the chief front and center and afterward get interest installments until the security develops. At development, investors are reimbursed the head. The chief doesn't increment in esteem over the long run the manner in which a stock would, however fixed-pay protections ought to turn out unsurprising revenue.

Alternative investment. Elective speculations is a catchall resource class for anything that is not money, values, or fixed pay. Land, valuable metals, digital money, and shared advances are elective ventures.

Bonds (otherwise called fixed-interest stocks). These are a type of IOU gave by legislatures and organizations when they need to get cash from investors. They pay a proper degree of interest, with higher-risk borrowers paying more in interest than lower-risk borrowers.

Property. Whether private or business, property has a decent record in giving a monetary return that beats expansion. Assets can either become involved with physical 'blocks and mortar' or purchase partakes in property improvement or land speculation organizations. Reserves for the most part center around business property, however some get involved with private property too.

Commodities. There is an immense assortment of items exchanged on worldwide business sectors. The reach incorporates oil and gas; valuable metals like gold and silver; modern metals like copper and iron; and 'delicate' farming wares like wheat, rice and soya. Very much like offers and securities, item costs rise and fall because of market interest, and assets can exploit this.

These resource classes can act in an unexpected way. There are times when some will get along admirably and others ineffectively. Every one of them are inclined to periodic air pockets and crashes, which makes it challenging to sum up something over the top.

Chapter 8

Investment strategy

What Is an Investment Strategy?

The term venture system alludes to a bunch of standards intended to assist a singular investor with accomplishing their monetary and investment objectives. This plan is the very thing that directs a investor's choices in light of objectives, risk resilience, and future requirements for capital.

They can differ from moderate (where they follow a generally safe system where the emphasis is on abundance security) while others are profoundly forceful (looking for fast development by zeroing in on capital appreciation).

Investors can utilize their systems to form their own portfolios or do as such through a monetary expert. Methodologies aren't static, and that implies they should be checked on intermittently as conditions change.

1 - Passive and Active Strategies
The latent methodology includes purchasing and holding stocks and not oftentimes managing them to stay away from higher exchange costs. They accept they can't outflank the market because of its unpredictability; subsequently inactive techniques will generally be safer. Then again, dynamic methodologies include successive trading. They accept they can beat the market and can acquire returns than a typical investor would.

2 - Growth Investing (Short-Term and Long-Term Investments)

Investors picked the holding period in view of the worth they need to make in their portfolio. On the off chance that investors accept that an organization will fill before very long and the characteristic worth of a stock will go up, they will put resources into such organizations to fabricate their corpus esteem. This is otherwise called development contributing.

Then again, assuming investors accept that an organization will convey great worth in a little while, they will go for transient holding. The holding time frame additionally relies on the inclination of investors. For instance, how soon they believe that cash should purchase a house, school instruction for youngsters, retirement plans, and so on.

3 - Value Investing

Esteem putting methodology includes putting resources into the organization by taking a gander at its characteristic worth on the grounds that such organizations are underestimated by the securities exchange. The thought behind putting resources into such organizations is that when the market goes for adjustment, it will address the incentive for such underestimated organizations, and the cost will then, at that point, shoot up, leave investors with significant yields when they sell.

4 - Income Investing
This sort of methodology centers around creating cash pay from stocks as opposed to putting resources into stocks that main increment the worth of your portfolio. There are two kinds of money pay which a investor can acquire -
(1) Dividend
(2) Fixed interest pay from bonds.

Investors who are searching for consistent pay from speculations select such a procedure.

5 - Dividend Growth Investing
In this kind of speculation procedure, the investor pays special attention to organizations that reliably delivered a profit consistently. Organizations that have a history of delivering profits reliably are steady and less unstable contrasted with different organizations and intend to expand their profit payout consistently. The investors reinvest such profits and advantage from intensifying over the long haul.

6 - Contrarian Investing
This kind of technique permits investors to purchase loads of organizations at the hour of the down market. This technique focusses on purchasing at low and selling

at high. The margin time in the securities exchange
is as a rule at the hour of downturn, wartime, catastrophe, and so forth. Nonetheless, investors shouldn't simply purchase loads of any organization during free time. They ought to pay special attention to organizations that have the ability to develop esteem and have a marking that forestalls admittance to their opposition.

7 - Indexing
This kind of venture methodology permits investors to put a little piece of stocks in a market record. These can be S&P 500, shared reserves, trade exchanged reserves.

Chapter 9

Knowing how to work out financial ratios

What are Financial Ratios?

Monetary proportions are made with the utilization of mathematical qualities taken from fiscal summaries to acquire significant data about an organization. The numbers tracked down on an organization's fiscal summaries - monetary record, pay explanation, and income proclamation - are utilized to perform quantitative examination and survey an organization's liquidity, influence, development, edges, productivity, paces of return, valuation, and that's just the beginning.

Monetary proportions are gathered into the accompanying classifications:

- Liquidity ratios
- Leverage ratios
- Efficiency ratios
- Profitability ratios
- Market value ratios

1. Liquidity Ratios
Liquidity ratios are monetary proportions that action an organization's capacity to reimburse both short-and long haul commitments. Normal liquidity proportions incorporate the accompanying:

The ongoing proportion estimates an organization's capacity to take care of transient liabilities with current resources:

Current ratio = Current asset/Current liabilities

The basic analysis ratio estimates an organization's capacity to take care of momentary liabilities with speedy resources:

Basic analysis ratio = Current resources - Inventories/Current liabilities

The money ratio estimates an organization's capacity to take care of momentary liabilities with endlessly cash reciprocals:

Cash ratio = Endlessly cash reciprocals/Current Liabilities

The working income ratio is a proportion of the times an organization can take care of current liabilities with the money produced in a given period:

Working income ratio = Operating income/Current liabilities

2. Leverage Financial Ratios

Leverage ratios measure how much capital that comes from obligation. All in all, leverage monetary ratios are utilized to assess an organization's obligation levels. Normal influence ratios incorporate the accompanying:

The obligation ratio estimates the general measure of an organization's resources that are given from obligation:

Obligation ratio = Total liabilities/Total assets

The obligation to value ratio ascertains the heaviness of complete obligation and monetary liabilities against investors' value:

Obligation to value ratio = Total liabilities/Shareholder's value

The interest inclusion ratio demonstrates the way that effectively an organization can pay its advantage costs:

Interest inclusion ratio = Operating pay/Interest costs

The obligation administration inclusion ratio uncovers how effectively an organization can pay its obligation commitments:

Obligation administration inclusion ratio = Operating pay/Total obligation administration

3. Proficiency Ratios
Effectiveness ratios, otherwise called action monetary ratios, are utilized to gauge how well an organization is using its resources and assets. Normal proficiency ratios include:

The resource turnover ratio estimates an organization's capacity to produce deals from resources:

Resource turnover ratio = Net deals/Average absolute assets

The stock turnover ratio estimates how often an organization's stock is sold and supplanted over a given period:

Stock turnover ratio = Cost of merchandise sold/Average stock

The records receivable turnover ratio estimates how often an organization can transform receivables into cash over a given period:

Receivables turnover ratio = Net credit deals/Average records receivable

The days deals in stock ratio estimates the typical number of days that an organization clutches stock prior to offering it to clients:

Days deals in stock ratio = 365 days/Inventory turnover ratio

4. Productivity Ratios
Productivity ratios measure an organization's capacity to create pay comparative with income, monetary record resources, working expenses, and value. Normal benefit monetary proportions incorporate the accompanying:

The net edge ratio looks at the net benefit of an organization to its net deals to show how much benefit an organization makes subsequent to paying its expense of products sold:

Net edge ratio = Gross benefit/Net deals

The working edge ratio looks at the working pay of an organization to its net deals to decide working proficiency:

Working edge ratio = Operating pay/Net deals

The profit from resources ratio estimates how productively an organization is utilizing its resources for create benefit:

Return on resources ratio = Net pay/Total resources

The profit from value ratio estimates how effectively an organization is utilizing its value to produce benefit:

Return on value ratio = Net pay/Shareholder's value

5. Market Value Ratios

Market esteem ratios are utilized to assess the offer cost of an organization's stock. Normal market esteem proportions incorporate the accompanying:

The book esteem per share ratio computes the per-share worth of an organization in view of the value accessible to investors:

Book esteem per share ratio = (Shareholder's value - Preferred value)/Total normal offers extraordinary

The profit yield ratio estimates how much profits ascribed to investors comparative with the market esteem per share:

Profit yield ratio = Dividend per share/Share cost

The profit per share ratio estimates how much overall gain procured for each offer remarkable:

Income per share ratio = Net profit/Total offers extraordinary

The cost profit ratio looks at an organization's portion cost to its income per share:

Cost income ratio = Share cost/Earnings per share

Chapter 10

Figuring out how to protect capital

What Is Preservation of Capital? Protection of capital is a moderate venture system where the essential objective is to save capital and forestall misfortune in a portfolio. This technique requires interest in the most secure transient instruments, for example, Treasury bills and endorsements of store.

Protection of capital is likewise alluded to as capital safeguarding.

Kinds of Capital Preservation Investments
Capital protection protections are related with negligible gamble.

Some capital conservation speculations — including investment accounts, CDs, government bonds and depository charges — are safeguarded by the Federal Deposit Insurance Corporation (FDIC) up to $250,000.

Choosing the right resources for safeguard your head and protect capital relies upon your own gamble resilience and monetary objectives.

Capital protection protections include:
- High return investment accounts
- Depository bills
- Metropolitan bonds
- U.S. investment funds securities
- Endorsements of stores (CDs)
- Deadline reserves
- Annuities

Securities and CDs are generally safe investment funds devices. Both work by holding cash in a record for a particular time frame. At the point when that time is up, your safeguarded chief is returned alongside some interest.

Financing costs for civil bonds can average around 3%. A one-year CD loan fee midpoints around 0.64 percent a year.

High return bank accounts opened on the web or through a credit association can procure 0.5 to 1 percent a year. By correlation, a conventional bank account procures around 0.06 percent a year.

Depository bonds, notes and bills are totally supported by the U.S. government. These three choices procure interest in somewhat various ways and mature at various times.

For instance, Treasury notes mature inside two to 10 years, while Treasury bonds as a rule require no less than 10 years to develop. Depository bills have the speediest circle back, with a development of one year or less.

At long last, annuities are a protection item that can be utilized for capital conservation. They ensure a revenue stream for a specific period and are frequently attached to current financing costs.

There are many kinds of annuities, however they can be a perplexing method for shielding your cash. Make a point to explore your choices prior to buying one cautiously. Quick and fixed annuities will more often than not be well known choices for head security.

What Is the Goal of Capital Preservation?

The goal of capital protection is to defend your cash, ordinarily for the present moment. Development isn't the essential objective.

As individuals age, safeguarding money and capital turns out to be more significant. Time skylines are more limited, giving investors a more modest window to develop assets and bounce back from misfortunes.

Monetary specialists suggest decreasing your gamble with age. Market unpredictability is a greater danger as you close to retirement since you really want the cash soon — not in 30 years, similar to a more youthful investor.

That is the reason resources required inside the following three to seven years ought to be contributed safely, with an emphasis on safeguarding head.

So, capital conservation surrenders huge possible returns in return for security and steadiness.

Chapter 11

Figuring out capital construction of an organization as an investor

Capital construction alludes to the particular blend of obligation and value used to back an organization's resources and tasks. According to a corporate point of view, value addresses a more costly, extremely durable wellspring of capital with more noteworthy monetary adaptability. Obligation, then again, addresses a less expensive, limited to-development capital source that legitimately commits the organization to fixed, guaranteed cash outpourings with the need to renegotiate sometime not too far off at an obscure expense.

An organization's capital construction is the consequence of such funding choices that might be directed by capital design strategies or targets set by the executives and the board. Capital construction is likewise the consequence of such factors as organization size and development, which impact the funding choices an organization might have accessible. Other than value and obligation issuance, capital construction can likewise be altogether impacted by consolidation and securing (M&A) action, which can be funded with cash, getting, share presumption or potentially obligation suspicion notwithstanding continues from divestitures and resource deals. Capital design is additionally impacted over the long run by the organization's activities, which could consume or produce cash, and by the executives choices with respect to profits and offer buybacks.

Since we are thinking about how an organization limits its general expense of capital, the emphasis here is available upsides of obligation and value. Subsequently, capital design is likewise impacted by changes in the market worth of an organization's protections over the long haul, especially the offer cost.

We will generally consider capital design the consequence of a cognizant choice by the executives, yet it is quite difficult. For instance, unmanageable obligation, or monetary misery, can emerge in light of the fact that an organization's capital design strategy was excessively forceful, however it can likewise happen in light of the fact that working outcomes or possibilities weaken startlingly.

This perusing audits a portion of the key variables influencing capital design, including the accompanying:

Organization life cycle: Companies ordinarily advance after some time from cash buyers to cash generators, with diminishing business risk and expanding obligation limit.

Cost of capital: From a hypothetical point of view, the executive looks to expand investor esteem and decides an ideal capital construction to limit the organization's weighted typical expense of capital (WACC). "Ideal capital construction" includes a compromise between the advantages of higher influence, which incorporate the expense deductibility of interest and the lower cost of obligation comparative with value, and the expenses of higher influence, which incorporate higher gamble for every capital supplier and the expected expenses of monetary pain.

Funding contemplations: From a functional point of view, organization the executives might think about a few elements in capital design choices and the utilization of influence.

Contending partner interests: In trying to augment investor esteem, organization the executives might settle on capital design choices that are not in that frame of mind of different partners, like debtholders, providers, clients, or representatives.

How would you get knowledge into an organization's capital construction?
A significant asset in surveying capital construction is an organization's monetary record, which organizes an organization's resources and liabilities including value and obligation — permitting you to perceive the amount of the capital design each of these

addresses. However both value and obligation furnish a business with assets, they each have their own separate assets and shortcomings. Capital designs that favor value over obligation or the other way around recommend qualities in a business, which will illuminate who that business requests to.

The proportion of an organization's obligation to value (at times communicated as D/E) can be useful in rapidly implying liability. By setting an organization's obligation with regards to investor value, it's more straightforward to perceive how turned an organization is and whether there would be sufficient value to cover obligation commitments if vital. The most common way of recognizing capital design is genuinely straightforward and objective yet frequently prompts more subjective or emotional evaluations of an organization in light of whether a investor, accomplice or specialist co-op considers it to accommodate their gamble resistance or their apparent ideal capital design.

For what reason do investors have to know an organization's capital construction?

An expected investor, acquirer or specialist co-op has to be familiar with an organization's obligation liabilities or value structure for various reasons. One significant explanation is to survey their endeavor esteem or foresee the monetary effect existing commitments might have on an organization later down the line. Understanding an organization's capital construction can likewise be helpful in deciding the sorts of monetary administrations they might require now or later on. On account of existing obligation, data on the kind of obligation, its development timetables and loan costs can be an extra wellspring of understanding.

Chapter 12

The investor and inflation

For buyers, inflation implies greater costs on labor and products, and the gamble of a deficiency of buying power in the event that their pay neglects to keep up. On the other hand, a decrease in costs is known as deflation.

Steady deflation can increase joblessness and sabotage the monetary framework as well as the more extensive economy by making it more challenging to support obligation. The U.S. Central bank is focusing on a 2% normal inflation rate after some time as generally steady with its double order to advance value soundness and greatest work.

Sharp deviations from an unobtrusive expansion rate in either bearing present difficulties for investors as well as purchasers. That is on the grounds that they have the potential for critical financial disturbance. They likewise significantly affect different resource classes.

Inflation has turned into a fixation for proficient investors and shoppers the same in 2022.

Worries about the financial effect of rising costs — and their cure, higher loan fees — have burdened stocks, diving the S&P 500 into a bear market briefly in June.

From the outset, it may not be clear whether rising costs are awful for stocks. While raised expansion can have serious unfortunate results for the more extensive economy, it's anything but a debacle for investors.

How Does Inflation Work?
Inflation is the wide, continuous expansion in costs across a whole economy. At the point when costs rise, expansion brings down the buying influence of cash.

National banks consider a moderate measure of inflation important to support financial development. The Fed goes for the gold term focus of 2% yearly expansion development, for instance, as estimated by the center individual utilization uses cost record (PCE).

Nonetheless, when inflation runs excessively high for a really long time, it's a certain sign that an economy is overheating.

Hot inflation demonstrates that buyer request is outperforming supply, driving costs higher — alleged request pull inflation. On the other hand, inventory network issues might make products more costly — that is cost-push inflation.

One way or the other, an overheating economy will ultimately push costs to where spending declines. Furthermore, while spending falls, the economy can without much of a stretch tumble into a downturn. As a matter of fact, an overheated economy has been one of the most widely recognized downturn triggers in the U.S. since World War II.

Chapter 13

investor versus speculation

investors and dealers go ahead with on reasonable plans of action as they endeavor to benefit from exchanges they make in the business sectors. The degree of hazard embraced in the exchanges is the principal distinction among effective financial planning and speculating.

Whenever an individual enjoys cash with the assumption that the undertaking will return a benefit, they are financial planning. In this situation, the endeavor puts together the choice with respect to a sensible judgment made after a careful examination of the sufficiency that the undertaking has a decent likelihood of progress.

However, imagine a scenario where a similar individual burns through cash on an endeavor that shows a high likelihood of disappointment. For this situation, they are speculating. The achievement or disappointment relies fundamentally upon possibility, or on wild (outer) powers or occasions.

Investing
Putting can come in various structures — through money related, time, or energy-based techniques. In the monetary feeling of the term, contributing means the trading of protections, for example, stocks, securities, trade exchanged reserves (ETFs), common assets, and different other monetary items.

investors desire to create pay or benefit through a good profit from their capital by taking on a normal or less than ideal measure of hazard. Pay can be as the fundamental resource valuing in esteem, in occasional profits or interest installments, or in the full return of their spent capital.

Most frequently, contributing is the demonstration of purchasing and holding a resource as long as possible. To group as a drawn out holding, the investor should claim the resource for something like one year.

We should think about a huge stable worldwide organization to act as an illustration of money management. This organization might deliver a predictable profit that builds every year, and it might have a low business risk. A investor might decide to put resources into this organization over the long haul to make a good profit from their capital while facing somewhat okay. Also, the investor might add a few comparable organizations across various businesses to their portfolio to broaden and additionally bring down their gamble.

Investigation and exploration is a critical piece of the speculation cycle. It includes assessing various resources, areas, and examples or patterns that happen on the lookout. investors can utilize apparatuses like essential or specialized examination to pick their venture methodologies or plan their portfolios. By utilizing central examination, investors can figure out what variables influence the worth of protections, from microeconomic to macroeconomic elements. Specialized examination, then again, utilizes measurable patterns, for example, security costs and volumes to track down amazing open doors on the lookout.

investors have numerous choices accessible for them to put away their cash. Money market funds give investors admittance to various protections. By opening a record, a investor consents to set aside installments and afterward puts orders through the firm. The resources and pay have a place with the investors, while the business takes a commission for working with the exchanges. With new innovation, investors can now contribute with robo-counsels, as well. These are mechanized speculation organizations that utilization a calculation to concoct a venture system in view of investors' objectives and chance resilience.

Speculating
Speculating is the demonstration of placing cash into monetary undertakings with a high likelihood of disappointment. Speculating looks for unusually

significant yields from wagers that can go for sure. While speculating is compared to betting, it isn't the very same, as speculators attempt to pursue an informed choice on the course of their exchanges. In any case, the intrinsic speculative gamble engaged with the exchange will in general be fundamentally better than expected.

These dealers purchase protections with the comprehension that they will be held for just a brief period prior to selling. They may much of the time into and out of a position.

To act as an illustration of a speculative exchange, consider an unpredictable junior gold mining organization with an equivalent opportunity over a shorter period of time of soaring from another mother lode disclosure or failing. With no report from the organization, investors would will more often than not avoid such a hazardous exchange. Be that as it may, a few examiners might accept the lesser gold mining organization will strike gold and may purchase its stock on a hunch. This hunch and the resulting action by investors is called speculation.

Speculative exchanging has its ruins. At the point when there are expanded assumptions for development or cost activity for a specific resource class or area, values will rise. At the point when this occurs, exchanging volume increments, in the end prompting an air pocket. This occurred with the dotcom bubble. Interest in Internet organizations filled dramatically in the last part of the 1990s, with valuations rising quickly. The market slumped after 2001, making significant tech organizations lose a major lump of their worth, with numerous others being cleared out.

Chapter 14

The investor and stock market fluctuations

What is the stock market?

The stock market is where purchasers and dealers exchange such monetary assets as bonds, monetary standards and values. One of the most well known resources is shares. They're units of possession in an organization, and investors get them to get profits from an organization or make gets back from future cost climbs.

Organizations likewise offer their portions to raise capital. An organization can't exchange on the financial exchange without at least capital, investors and different prerequisites.

Representatives assume a vital part in the financial exchange. They're qualified experts who acquaint purchasers with merchants and execute exchanges for commission. Organizations and people hoping to put resources into the financial exchange ought to go through a specialist.

When does the stock market fluctuate?

Like some other items, the cost of offers relies on organic market. Costs rise when the stockpile of offers for buy isn't sufficient to fulfill the need of investors; they fall when less investors are keen on purchasing shares.

For what reason does the stock market fluctuate?

Share costs commonly go all over in view of the organic market. In any case, they're likewise affected by these variables:

- Data: When exchanging offers, purchasers and venders really look at the most recent news on an organization or an industry. Their view of the data might contrast, which will likewise impact their choice to trade. For example, on the off chance that an organization declares plans to extend universally, the likely flood in benefits might ignite investors' advantage and the offer cost might take off.

- The economy: The presentation of a nation's or alternately locale's economy, most prominently GDP (GDP) and loan costs, can affect share costs. As the GDP rises, creation based enterprises draw in additional speculation and interest for shares. Assuming loan costs increase, organizations need to pay out more cash to get, making net revenues psychologist and offers to lose their allure.

- The organization's monetary wellbeing: Listed organizations are expected to routinely distribute their budget summaries. The benefit and misfortune they incorporate can assist investors and investors with settling on exchanging choices. In the event that results introductions show positive figures, interest for offers could rise and influence their cost.

- External occasions: Impressions about an organization's presentation can weigh vigorously on the interest for its portions. Non-monetary occasions like conflicts, pandemics and catastrophic events give investors vulnerability about dangers to the capital put resources into the organizations and enterprises they influence.

Chapter 15

The investor and his Advisors

An investment advisor is an individual or organization who is paid for giving exhortation about protections to their clients. Albeit the terms sound comparative, speculation counsels are not equivalent to monetary guides and ought not be confounded. The term monetary counsel is a conventional term that typically alludes to a dealer (or, to utilize the specialized term, an enlisted delegate). Paradoxically, the term venture consultant is a legitimate term that alludes to an individual or organization that is enlisted as such with either the Securities and Exchange Commission or a state protections controller. Normal names for venture consultants incorporate resource directors, speculation guides, venture administrators, portfolio chiefs, and abundance supervisors. Speculation consultant agents are people who work for and offer guidance for enrolled venture counselors.

How Investment Advisors Work
Investment advisors fill in as experts inside the monetary business by giving direction to clients in return for explicit expenses. Speculation guides owe a guardian obligation to their clients and are expected to put their clients' advantages first consistently.

For instance, investment advisors should guarantee that clients' exchanges are given need over their own and that any proposals made to clients are very much custom fitted to those clients' necessities, inclinations, and monetary conditions. Venture counselors should likewise be mindful so as to stay away from any genuine or saw irreconcilable situations.

One manner by which investment advisors try to limit genuine or saw irreconcilable circumstances is through their pay structure. Speculation guides are paid through expenses which make their own prosperity be connected to that of the client.

Choosing a advisor
Investment advisors are expected to act to your greatest advantage and not put their advantage in front of yours. Simultaneously, the manner in which counsels bring in cash makes a few struggles with your inclinations. You ought to comprehend and get some information about these contentions since they can influence the venture exhortation they give. Leading a careful investigation into a consultant's

administrations, expense plans, and speculation contributions will assist you with choosing a counsel equipped for serving your venture goals.

Prior to choosing an advisor, you ought to consider:

- what administrations and items you really want,
- what administrations and items the consultant can give,
- any impediments on what administrations and items the counselor can give,
- the amount you will pay for administrations and exchanges,
- how the counselor gets compensated,
- what irreconcilable situations the guide might have while offering you speculation guidance, and

- whether the guide has lawful or disciplinary history and, provided that this is true, for what kind of lead.

The administrations and guidance your counselor gives and what expenses you pay will eventually rely upon the agreement you haggle with your consultant.

Chapter 16

Interesting points about per-share profit

Income per share (EPS) is determined as an organization's benefit separated by the extraordinary portions of its not unexpected stock. The subsequent number fills in as a mark of an organization's benefit. It is normal for an organization to report EPS that is adapted to phenomenal things and potential offer weakening.

The higher an organization's EPS, the more productive it is viewed as.

Equation and Calculation for Earnings Per Share (EPS)

Income per share esteem is determined as overall gain (otherwise called benefits or profit) partitioned by accessible offers. A more refined estimation changes the numerator and denominator for shares that could be made through choices, convertible obligation, or warrants. The numerator of the situation is likewise more significant on the off chance that it is adapted to proceeding with activities.

To work out an organization's EPS, the monetary record and pay proclamation are utilized to find the period-end number of normal offers, profits paid on favored stock (if any), and the overall gain or income. It is more precise to utilize a weighted typical number of normal offers over the detailing term on the grounds that the quantity of offers can change after some time.

Any stock profits or parts that happen should be reflected in the estimation of the weighted typical number of offers remarkable. A few information sources improve on the computation by utilizing the quantity of offers remarkable toward the finish of a period.

How Is EPS Used?
Income per share is quite possibly of the main measurement utilized while deciding a company's benefit on a flat out premise. It is likewise a significant part of computing the cost to-profit (P/E) proportion, where the E in P/E alludes to EPS. By partitioning an organization's portion value by its profit per share, a investor can see the worth of a stock as far as how much the market will pay for every dollar of income.

EPS is one of the numerous pointers you could use to pick stocks. Assuming you have a premium in stock exchanging or effective money management, your following stage is to pick a merchant that works for your venture style.

Looking at EPS in outright terms might not have a lot significance to investors since normal investors don't have direct admittance to the profit. All things being equal, investors will contrast EPS and the offer cost of the stock to decide the worth of profit and how investors feel about future development.

EPS From Continuing Operations
An organization began the year with 500 stores and had an EPS of $5.00. Nonetheless, expect that this organization shut down 100 stores over that period and finished the year with 400 stores. An examiner will need to understand what the EPS was for simply

the 400 stores the organization intends to go on within the following time frame.

In this model, that could build the EPS on the grounds that the 100 shut down stores were maybe losing money. By assessing EPS from proceeding with activities, an expert is better ready to contrast earlier execution with current execution

EPS and Capital
A significant part of EPS that is frequently overlooked is the capital that is expected to create the profit (net gain) in the computation. Two organizations could produce a similar EPS, however one could do as such with less net resources; that organization would be more proficient at utilizing its money to create pay and, any remaining things being equivalent, would be a "superior" organization regarding productivity. A

metric that can be utilized to distinguish more effective organizations is the profit from value (ROE).

EPS and Dividends
In spite of the fact that EPS is broadly utilized as a method for following an organization's exhibition, investors don't have direct admittance to those benefits. A piece of the income might be conveyed as a profit, however all or a part of the EPS can be held by the organization. Investors, through their agents on the top managerial staff, would need to change the piece of EPS that is dispersed through profits to get to a greater amount of those benefits.

EPS and Price-to-Earnings (P/E)
Making a correlation of the P/E proportion inside an industry gathering can be useful, however unexpectedly. Despite the fact that it appears to be a

stock that costs more comparative with its EPS when contrasted with companions may be "exaggerated," the inverse will in general be the standard. No matter what its verifiable EPS, investors will pay something else for a stock in the event that it is normal to develop or outflank its friends. In a buyer market, it is typical for the stocks with the most noteworthy P/E proportions in a stock record to outflank the normal of different stocks in the file.

What Is a Good EPS?
What considers a decent EPS will rely upon elements like the new execution of the organization, the exhibition of its rivals, and the assumptions for the examiners who follow the stock. Some of the time, an organization could report developing EPS, yet the stock could decrease in cost on the off chance that

examiners were anticipating a considerably bigger number.

In like manner, a contracting EPS figure could regardless prompt a cost increment on the off chance that experts were anticipating a much more dreadful outcome. It is vital to constantly pass judgment on EPS comparable to the organization's portion cost, like by taking a gander at the organization's P/E or income yield.